Achieving Guitar Artistry

Triads

by William Bay

MEL BAY ®

Exclusive Sales Agent: Mel Bay Publications, Inc.
www.melbay.com

Preface

This is a book for the ears and for the hands. Playing harmonized scales in triad form is extremely helpful for the progressing guitarist. First, you will become acquainted with the harmonic sound of each key. You will also develop a sense of harmonic and melodic voice leading. I personally have found that by daily practice of these etudes I am able to hear melodies and harmonies thus enabling me to improvise or compose freely in any key.

I have inserted some fingering and string numbering but I have kept it to a minimum for two reasons. First, most of these triads can be played in various places on the guitar fingerboard and I encourage you to experiment with different strings and positions. Second, I feel that note reading is essential to becoming a proficient guitarist and these etudes will also enhance your note reading abillity. See what fingering works for you!

I wrote these studies on successive strings. For a complete, thorough and exhaustive study of triads including the endless possibilties involving string skips, I recommend the 3 volume "Harmonic Mechanisms" set by the legendary jazz guitarist, George Van Eps (available from *www.melbay.com*). You can spend years working through that series!

As with everything I write, I wanted these studies to be fun to play and interesting melodically. Every effort has been made to compose these triad exercises on the member notes of the theoretical triads found within the scales; with the studies involving 7th chord extensions; however, I have let my personal taste guide my compositional decisions. I also chose to present these studies from tonic major to tonic minor instead of from tonic major to relative minor.

I find it helpful to play at least one key per day as a part of a daily practice routine. I hope you find these studies beneficial for your hands and ears and an enjoyable part of your guitar study and practice.

William Bay

Contents

Key	Page
C	4
Cm	7
G	10
Gm	13
D	16
Dm	19
A	22
Am	25
E	28
Em	31
B	34
Bm	37
F♯	40
F♯m	43
F	46
Fm	49
B♭	52
B♭m	55
E♭	58
E♭m	61
A♭	64
G♯m	67
D♭	70
C♯m	73

C-1

C-2

C-3

C-4

C-5

C-6

C-7

C-8

C-9

Cm-1

Cm-2

Cm-3

Cm-4

Cm-5

Cm-6

Cm-7

Cm-8

Cm-9

G-1

G-2

G-3

G-4

G-5

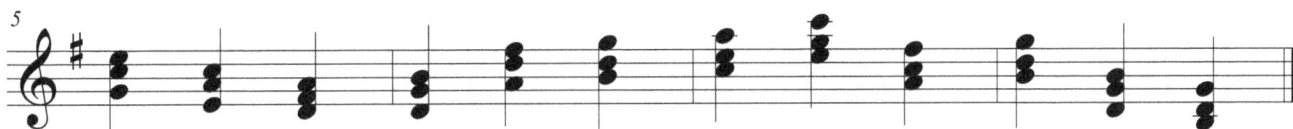

G-6

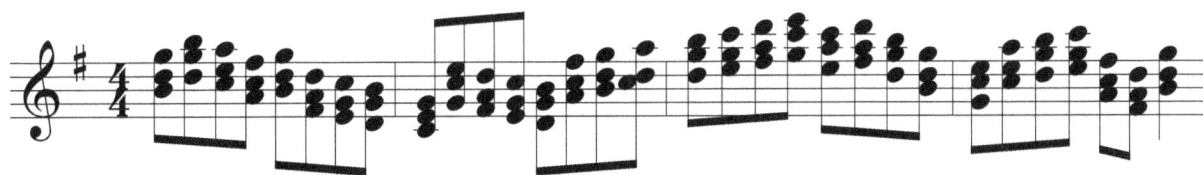

G-7

G-8

G-9

Gm-1

Gm-2

Gm-3

Gm-4

Gm-5

Gm-6

Gm-7

Gm-8

Gm-9

D-1

D-2

D-3

D-4

D-5

D-6

D-7

D-8

D-9

Dm-1

Dm-2

Dm-3

Dm-4

Dm-5

Dm-6

Dm-7

Dm-8

Dm-9

A-1

A-2

A-3

A-4

A-5

A-6

A-7

A-8

A-9

Am-1

Am-2

Am-3

Am-4

Am-5

Am-6

Am-7

Am-8

Am-9

E-1

E-2

E-3

E-4

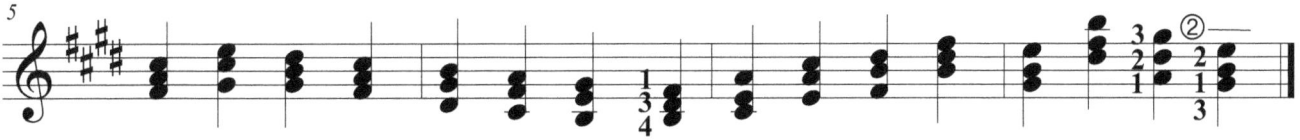

E-5

E-6

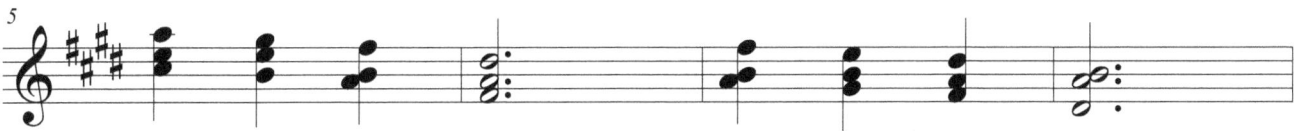

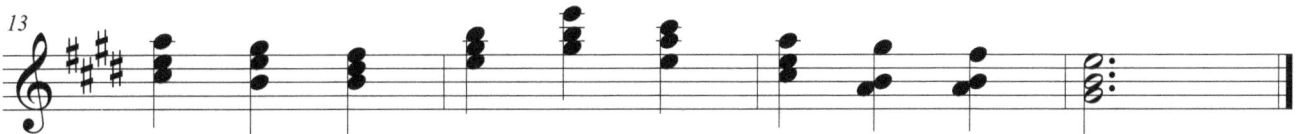

E-7

E-8

E-9

Em-1

Em-2

Em-3

Em-4

Em-5

Em-6

Em-7

Em-8

Em-9

B-1

B-2

B-3

B-4

B-5

B-6

B-7

B-8

B-9

Bm-1

Bm-2

Bm-3

Bm-4

Bm-5

Bm-6

Bm-7

Bm-8

Bm-9

F#-1

F#-2

F#-3

F#-4

F#-5

F#-6

F#-7

F#-8

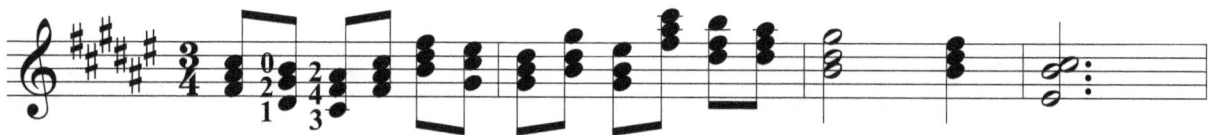

F#-9

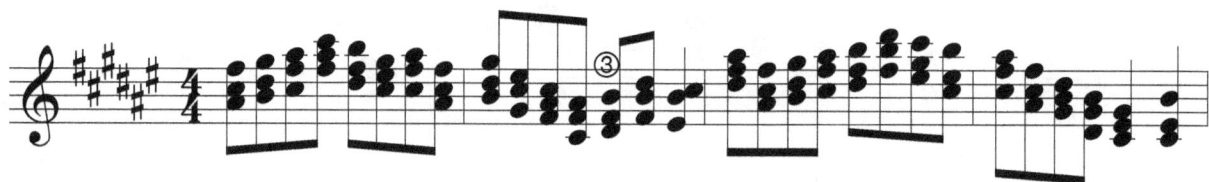

F#m-1

F#m-2

F#m-3

F#m-4

F#m-5

F#m-6

44

F#m-7

F#m-8

F#m-9

F-1

F-2

F-3

F-4

F-5

F-6

F-7

F-8

F-9

Fm-1

Fm-2

Fm-3

Fm-4

Fm-5

Fm-6

Fm-7

Fm-8

Fm-9

B♭-1

B♭-2

B♭-3

Bb-4

Bb-5

Bb-6

Bb-7

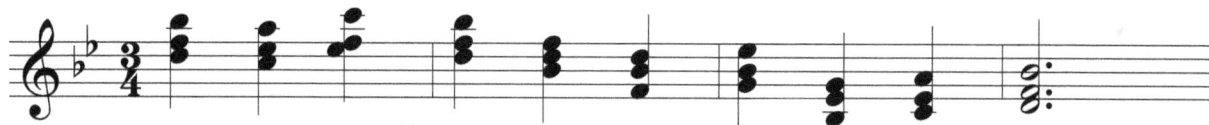

Bb-8

Bb-9

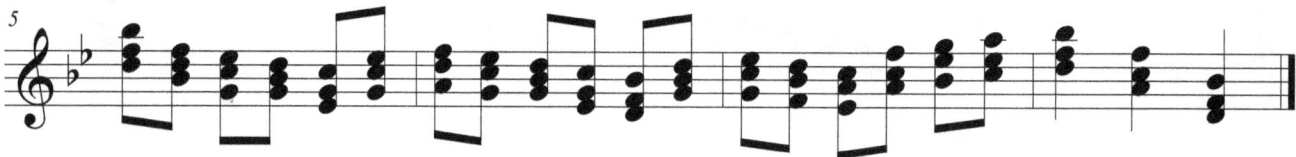

B♭m-1

B♭m-2

B♭m-3

Bbm-4

Bbm-5

Bbm-6

B♭m-7

B♭m-8

B♭m-9

Eb-1

Eb-2

Eb-3

Eb-4

Eb-5

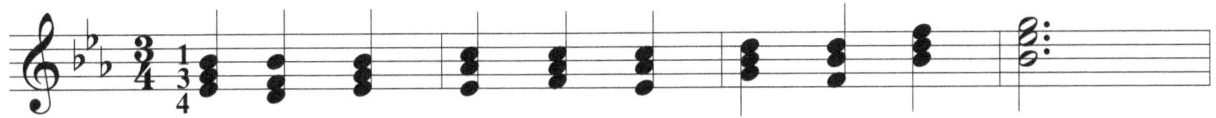

Eb-6

E♭-7

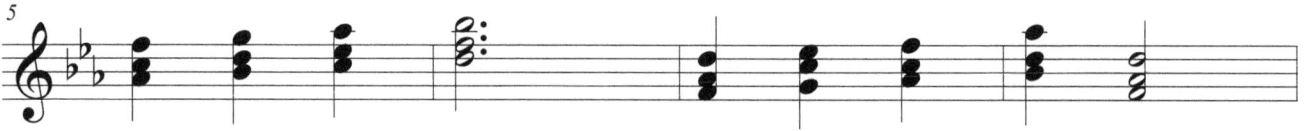

E♭-8

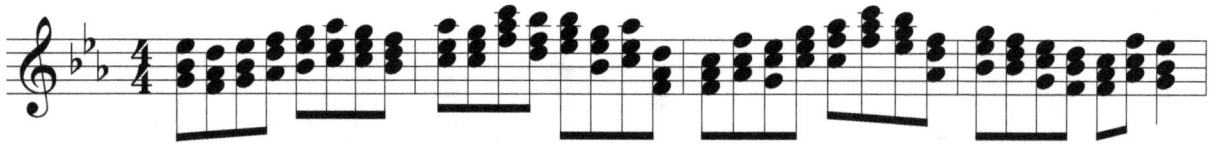

E♭-9

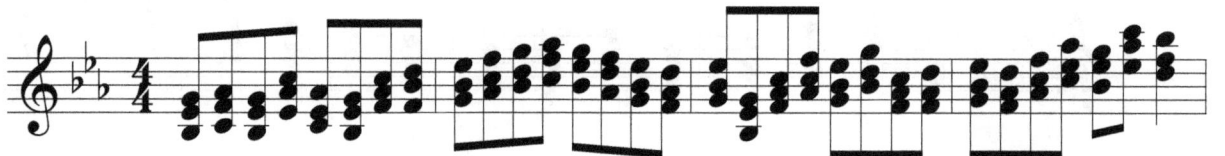

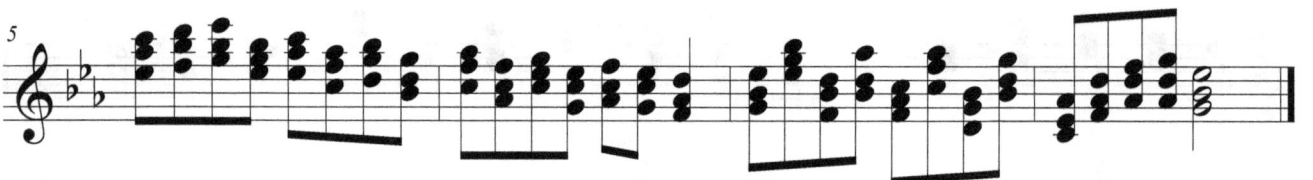

Ebm-1

Ebm-2

Ebm-3

Ebm-4

Ebm-5

Ebm-6

Ebm-7

Ebm-8

Ebm-9

Ab-1

Ab-2

Ab-3

Ab-4

Ab-5

Ab-6

Ab-7

Ab-8

Ab-9

G#m-1

G#m-2

G#m-3

G#m-4

G#m-5

G#m-6

G#m-7

G#m-8

G#m-9

Db-1

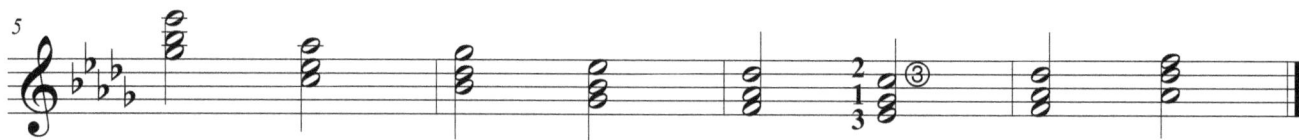

Db-2

Db-3

Db-4

Db-5

Db-6

Db-7

Db-8

Db-9

C#m-1

C#m-2

C#m-3

C#m-4

C#m-5

C#m-6

C#m-7

C#m-8

C#m-9

Other Recommended Books from Mel Bay

Achieving Guitar Artistry Series:
    WBM23 Linear Guitar Etudes
    WBM22 Concert Solos

George Van Eps: Harmonic Mechanisms for Guitar #1 (93667)

Complete Book of Guitar Chords, Scales & Arpeggios (94792)

Deluxe Guitar Scale Book (93282)

Extreme Warm-Ups & Chops Builders for Guitar (30510)

Building Guitar Finger Strength (99659)

Guitar Journals: Mastering the Fingerboard (20903)

Guitar Journals: Chords (20905)

Guitar Journals: Technique (20904)

Guitar Journals: Scales (20902)

Complete Book of Harmony, Theory & Voicing (95112)

MEL BAY®

WWW.MELBAY.COM